CAT BREEDS

SIAMESE CATS

BY ABBY DOTY

WWW.APEXEDITIONS.COM

Copyright © 2025 by Apex Editions, Mendota Heights, MN 55120. All rights reserved. No part of this book may be reproduced or utilized in any form or by any means without written permission from the publisher.

Apex is distributed by North Star Editions:
sales@northstareditions.com | 888-417-0195

Produced for Apex by Red Line Editorial.

Photographs ©: Shutterstock Images, cover, 1, 4–5, 6, 7, 8, 10–11, 13, 14, 15, 16–17, 18, 19, 20, 21, 22–23, 24–25, 26–27, 29

Library of Congress Control Number: 2024944887

ISBN
979-8-89250-315-0 (hardcover)
979-8-89250-353-2 (paperback)
979-8-89250-428-7 (ebook pdf)
979-8-89250-391-4 (hosted ebook)

Printed in the United States of America
Mankato, MN
012025

NOTE TO PARENTS AND EDUCATORS

Apex books are designed to build literacy skills in striving readers. Exciting, high-interest content attracts and holds readers' attention. The text is carefully leveled to allow students to achieve success quickly. Additional features, such as bolded glossary words for difficult terms, help build comprehension.

TABLE OF CONTENTS

CHAPTER 1
CLEVER CATS 4

CHAPTER 2
BREED HISTORY 10

CHAPTER 3
PRETTY AND PLAYFUL 16

CHAPTER 4
CAT CARE 22

COMPREHENSION QUESTIONS • 28
GLOSSARY • 30
TO LEARN MORE • 31
ABOUT THE AUTHOR • 31
INDEX • 32

CHAPTER 1

CLEVER CATS

A girl tosses a toy mouse across a room. Two Siamese cats run after it. One cat grabs the toy. He brings it back to the girl.

Siamese cats don't like being alone. So, many owners get two cats.

Siamese cats are smart. They tend to learn tricks quickly.

Next, the girl holds out her hand. Each cat gives her a high five. The girl hits a clicker. Then she has the cats do other tricks.

CLICKER TRAINING

When cats do tricks, owners can hit a clicker and give out treats. The cats learn that clicks mean they will get treats. Soon, the clicks are their own **rewards**.

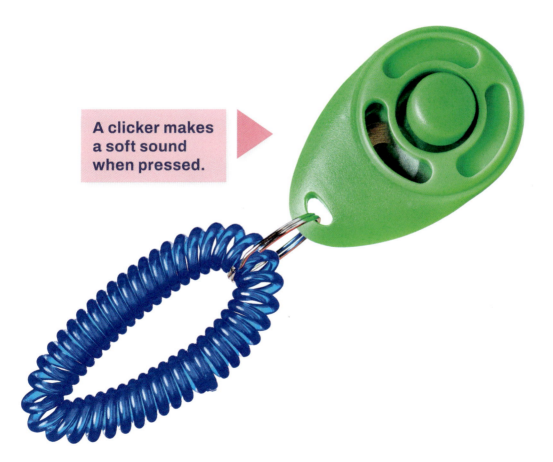

A clicker makes a soft sound when pressed.

After a few minutes of training, one cat curls up near a window. The other sits on the girl's lap. He meows happily.

FAST FACT
Siamese cats can be very vocal. They often meow to get attention.

◀ Most Siamese cats like to be cuddled and held.

CHAPTER 2

BREED HISTORY

Siamese cats are one of the oldest **breeds**. They came from an area called Siam. Long ago, many royals there owned cats.

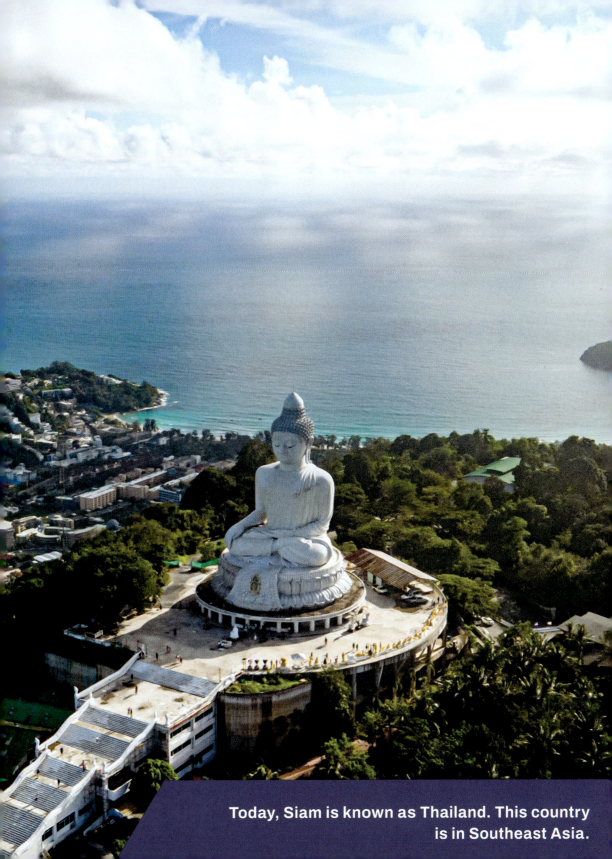

Today, Siam is known as Thailand. This country is in Southeast Asia.

In the late 1800s, the king of Siam gave two cats to an English **official**. The official brought the cats to England. People there loved how they looked. Soon, the breed spread to other parts of the world.

FAST FACT

Some Siamese cats lived at temples. People said the cats acted as guards.

Siamese cats have long bodies and sleek fur.

Old-style Siamese cats have big ears and round bodies.

In the mid-1900s, some people began **breeding** Siamese cats to have thinner bodies and pointier heads. Other people kept the old style.

DIFFERENT TYPES

Today, there are four types of Siamese cat. All types have short, silky fur. But the shape of their faces and ears varies. So does the length of their legs and tails.

Wedgehead Siamese cats have narrow faces. They became popular in the 1980s.

CHAPTER 3

PRETTY AND PLAYFUL

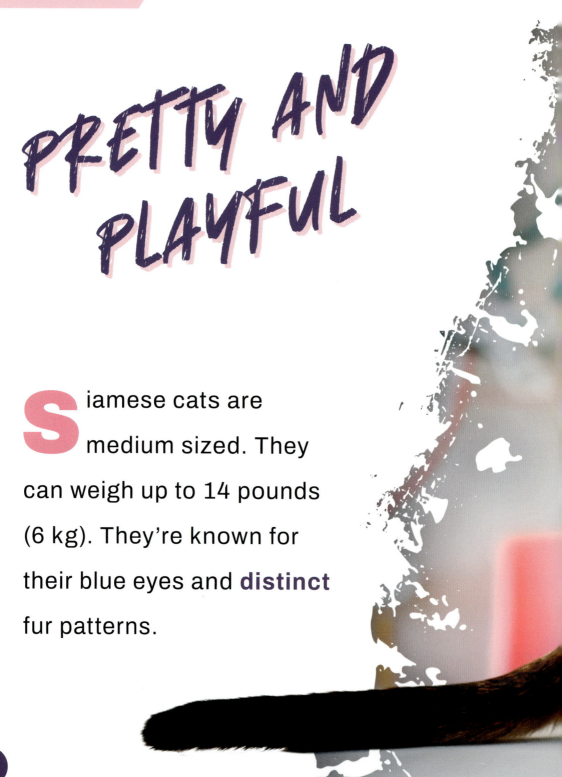

Siamese cats are medium sized. They can weigh up to 14 pounds (6 kg). They're known for their blue eyes and **distinct** fur patterns.

Most Siamese cats are about 13 inches (33 cm) long.

Light-colored fur covers most of a Siamese cat's body. But the cat's face, tail, ears, and legs have darker fur. These dark areas are called points.

Many Siamese cats have dark-brown or dark-gray points.

Because of their short fur, Siamese cats get cold easily. They may need sweaters or blankets.

FAST FACT

Siamese cats are born completely white. They get their colors after a few weeks.

Some Siamese cats can learn to walk on leashes.

Siamese cats have **lean** bodies. But they are still strong and athletic. They often run, jump, and climb. The cats also love to **explore**.

ACTIVE CATS

Siamese cats tend to have lots of **energy**. They get bored easily. When that happens, they may act out. Puzzles and toys can help the cats stay busy.

When bored, Siamese cats may rip curtains or scratch furniture.

CHAPTER 4

CAT CARE

Siamese cats need to be brushed once a week. But owners can brush them more often. The cats like the attention.

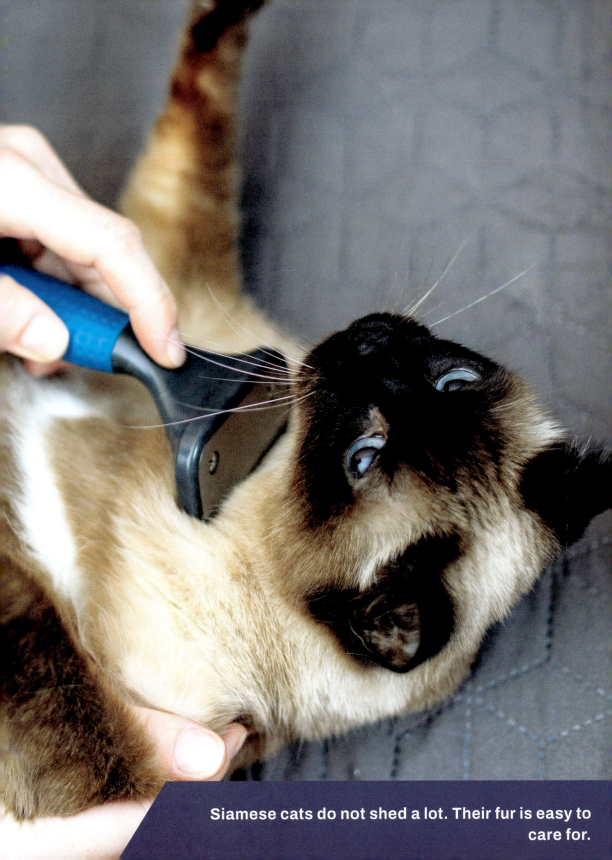

Siamese cats do not shed a lot. Their fur is easy to care for.

Most Siamese cats like to stay close to their owners.

Owners shouldn't leave Siamese cats alone for very long. The cats tend to be social. So, they often do well in households with children and other pets.

FAST FACT
Many Siamese cats get along with dogs.

25

Siamese cats need lots of **exercise**. Owners should play with their cats every day. Cat furniture can also help. For instance, many cats like to climb cat trees.

MEALTIME

Siamese cats tend to gain weight easily. And they often overeat. So, owners should not leave food sitting out all day. Instead, they can give cats a few small meals each day.

COMPREHENSION QUESTIONS

Write your answers on a separate piece of paper.

1. Write a few sentences explaining the main ideas of Chapter 3.

2. Would you like to own a Siamese cat? Why or why not?

3. How often should Siamese cats be brushed?

    A. once a year
    B. once a month
    C. once a week

4. Which owner would not be a good fit for a Siamese cat?

    A. an owner with several other pets
    B. an owner who spends lots of time at home
    C. an owner who is gone for most of the day

5. What does **vocal** mean in this book?

Siamese cats can be very vocal. They often meow to get attention.

- **A.** quiet
- **B.** noisy
- **C.** small

6. What does **athletic** mean in this book?

But they are still strong and athletic. They often run, jump, and climb.

- **A.** active
- **B.** friendly
- **C.** lazy

Answer key on page 32.

GLOSSARY

breeding

Raising animals, often in a way that creates certain looks or abilities.

breeds

Specific types of cats that have their own looks and abilities.

distinct

Easy to see or tell apart from others.

energy

The strength to move and be active.

exercise

The act of moving around and staying active.

explore

To search or move through an area.

lean

Thin and fit.

official

A person who works for the government.

rewards

Things given for doing a good job.

BOOKS

Clausen-Grace, Nicki. *Siamese*. Mankato, MN: Black Rabbit Books, 2020.

Jaycox, Jaclyn. *Read All About Cats*. North Mankato, MN: Capstone Publishing, 2021.

Pearson, Marie. *Cat Behavior*. Minneapolis: Abdo Publishing, 2024.

ONLINE RESOURCES

Visit **www.apexeditions.com** to find links and resources related to this title.

ABOUT THE AUTHOR

Abby Doty is a writer, editor, and booklover from Minnesota.

A
athletic, 20
attention, 9, 22

B
breeding, 14
breeds, 10, 12

C
clicker, 6–7

E
England, 12
exercise, 26
eyes, 16

F
fur, 15, 16, 18

K
king of Siam, 12

O
owners, 7, 22, 25–26

S
Siam, 10, 12
social, 25

T
toys, 4, 21
tricks, 6–7
types, 15

ANSWER KEY:
1. Answers will vary; 2. Answers will vary; 3. C; 4. C; 5. B; 6. A